SELECTED READINGS FROM

# AUGUSTINE *of* HIPPO

EDITED WITH INTRODUCTION BY
ROBERT VAN DE WEYER

Fleming H. Revell Company
Tarrytown, New York

**Fleming H. Revell Company Publishers,**
Tarrytown, New York
Copyright © 1991 Hunt & Thorpe
Text © 1991 by Robert van de Weyer
Originally published in the UK by Hunt and Thorpe 1991
First published in North America by Fleming Revell
ISBN 0-8007-7130-3

Illustrations by
Fred Apps, James Barton, Elvira Dadd and Vic Mitchell

All rights reserved. Except for brief quotations in
critical articles or reviews, no part of this book may be
reproduced in any manner without prior permission from the
publishers. Write to: Fleming H. Revell Company,
120 White Plains Road, Tarrytown, New York 10591.

Manufactured in the United Kingdom.

1 2 3 4 5 6 7 – 96 95 94 93 92 91

# CONTENTS

Eye of faith
Testing of faith
Peace

## 4. PRAYERS
Who, O Lord
O God, who knows our
  necessities
O God, you are close
Blessed are your saints

O Lord, you were rich
All things live in you
Our hearts are cold
In you we live
Let my soul praise you
Descend into my heart
You, Lord, are the light
Watch this night
Come Lord, set us on fire

# INTRODUCTION

*W*ithout doubt the most influential Christian writer of the first millennium of the Christian era, and possibly of all time, was Augustine of Hippo. Whether or not we are aware of his influence, the moral and spiritual attitudes of all of us have to some degree been moulded by his thoughts. The Protestant Reformers of the sixteenth century, such as Calvin and Luther, derived many of their ideas from him. The Roman Catholic church has long regarded him as one of the twin masters of Christian doctrine – the other being Thomas Aquinas. And in our century Christians seeking new insight and inspiration to revitalise the Church have found themselves plundering his prolific writings.

The story of Augustine's life, and especially of his dramatic conversion, is contained in his most famous work, *The Confessions*, which is one of the earliest Christian testimonies. He was born in 354 at Thegeste in North Africa, to a Christian mother, Monica, and a pagan father. At the age of 17 he went to Carthage to complete his education, and it is there that his spiritual and intellectual pilgrimage began. Under the influence of pagan philosophers he decided that the pursuit of 'wisdom' should be his primary goal; and to this end he read, amongst other works, the Bible. But he decided that Christian teaching was too simple to contain truth, and the style of the Scriptures too crude. He was soon drawn to the Manichaees, a gnostic sect which taught a strict dualism, in which goodness and evil are depicted as independent powers engaged in constant battle.

For nine years Augustine devoted himself to Manichaean philosophy. Throughout this period he was obsessed with his own sexuality, and the Manichaean dualism echoed his own attitude to sex. On the one hand he kept a mistress, who bore him a child, and he believed himself incapable of surviving without sexual relations. Yet on the other hand he readily accepted the Manichaean belief that all physical attachments, including sex, are sinful, since they enslave the human spirit. He tried in vain to suppress his sexual desire, hoping that through a strict routine of meditation and fasting he could overcome the sin of lust. But finally he concluded that Manichaeistic teaching was worthless, and he must look elsewhere.

In the meantime his career as a teacher of rhetoric had taken him to Rome and then to Milan where he encountered the great Christian bishop, Ambrose. He was enthralled by the eloquence of Ambrose's sermons, and impressed at the way Ambrose countered many of the intellectual objections to Christianity which Augustine himself held. Augustine, like many pagans, found the idea that God could be made flesh in Christ quite absurd and even contemptible, since that which is eternal and infinite could not be in any way contained within a temporal and finite body. Even the notion that God created men in his image appeared as a gross contradiction. Ambrose showed him that spirit and body are not locked in conflict, but that the material world, including the human body reflects the beauty of God, and can be made holy by His grace.

It was not only lust, but ambition which stirred Augustine's restless heart, and here too he found himself engaged in an inward tussle. On one occasion when he was on his way to deliver a lecture to a famous audience, he encountered a drunken beggar. He found himself envying the carefree happiness of the beggar who had nothing but a cask of wine while he who had such outward success could never enjoy even a single peaceful night, so anxious was he to add to his own reputation.

Gradually it dawned on him that his pursuit of wisdom had for all those years been flawed and because he had been unwilling to give up any earthly pleasure in the search, he had in effect been praying, 'Give me chastity, but not yet'. This realisation plunged him into the deepest anguish, knowing that the only means of knowing true inward peace was to entrust himself wholly to God's will. His description of this turmoil, and his eventual conversion to Christ, remains one of the most moving passages of all Christian literature. He was baptized by Ambrose in 366.

He returned to North Africa, where he formed a monastery – which was the foundation of one of the great medieval religious orders. In 391 he was ordained priest, and became bishop of Hippo five years later. He ruled that turbulent African diocese for thirty-four years, until his death in 430. His spiritual and theological teaching was to a great extent shaped by his own experience of conversion. His own struggle with sexuality and ambition are mirrored in his theology – and many have since blamed him for the negative attitude the Church has traditionally shown towards sex.

His teaching on sin led directly to his most controversial doctrine, that certain souls are predestined for salvation, whilst others are condemned to eternal punishment. He had himself found that individual effort and will-power could not free him from sin, and he regarded his own conversion as an unmerited gift from God. Since many others manifestly are not redeemed from sin, it followed that God must arbitrarily choose to save some and reject others. When his opponents objected that this was unjust, Augustine replied that justice would require all people to be condemned.

In their pure form, many of Augustine's ideas seem today too rigid and rigorous. But they are rooted not in some abstract theological scheme, but in a profound understanding of the human spirit. And it is the spiritual insight that makes his writings so inspiring. Apart from *The Confessions*, his finest works are his scriptural commentaries, especially on the Psalms, where the poetry of the psalmist carries him to the depths of the human soul. It is hardly surprising that many prayers, which continue to aid people in their own spiritual pilgrimage, have been culled from Augustine's writings.

Inevitably in a short book we can only skim the surface of his vast output. Nonetheless, so powerful was his pen that even a few passages can give a vivid impression of this extraordinary man's vision.

# 1

*The Confessions*, in which Augustine tells the story of his search for wisdom and conversion to Christ, is the most famous testimony in all Christian literature. In describing the spiritual anguish, and the moral chaos of his early life, Augustine shows no inhibitions. Although the book is quite long, containing numerous passages of theological and spiritual reflections, the essence of the story is in a few short and stunning chapters.

## CHILDHOOD SIN

As a youth I stole things of which I had plenty at home. And I did not even enjoy the things I stole, but simply took pleasure in the theft itself. For example, near our home there was a pear-tree whose fruit was rather dull and tasteless. At night I went with a group of friends and shook the tree, so the fruit fell to the ground. We carried away a huge load of fruit. But we didn't want to eat it, and simply gave it to the pigs. And, if we did take a few bites, it was not because we enjoyed the taste, but because we had a thrill in eating forbidden fruit.

## THE PRIDE OF SIN

The pleasure in that theft of fruit was in pretending to be like God, in a perverse and wicked manner. By breaking your law I could imagine myself above your law. Whilst in truth I was a slave to sin, I imagined myself free, able to commit sin without punishment. I took pleasure in breaking your law, not for any reward, but to fool myself that your law was beneath me.

# REJECTION OF SCRIPTURE

As I read the works of Cicero, I felt an overwhelming desire to turn from material pleasures, and pursue wisdom. I wanted to seek and embrace wisdom, wherever it might be found. Cicero, however, never mentioned the name of Christ. And, since from my earliest childhood I had been taught by my mother that Christ is my Saviour, drinking such an idea with my mother's milk, this made me cautious. So, impressed by Cicero to pursue wisdom, I decided to look for wisdom in the holy Scripture. Yet in the arrogance of my youth I was disappointed. I was too proud to understand the truth of Scripture, unwilling to bow my head in humility to its simple teaching. I imagined that wisdom could only be expressed in the lofty style of someone like Cicero. I despised the crudeness of the Bible.

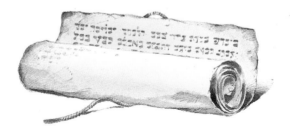

# THE FIRST DECISION

*I* came to Milan where I encountered Ambrose, the bishop, a man respected throughout the world as devout and holy. I can now see that God led me to him. This man of God welcomed me, as if he were my father. And I began to love him, not because of his teaching, but because of his warm and loving personality. I enjoyed hearing him preach, not in order to learn from what he said, but in order to admire and learn to imitate his eloquence. Indeed I still despised the doctrines he taught. Yet, by opening my heart to the sweetness of his speech, the truth of his teaching began to enter my soul, little by little. I began to see that Christianity, far from being an absurd nonsense as I had imagined, could be defended intellectually. He explained even the awkward parts of the Old Testament, so that my contempt for those primitive Hebrew prophets melted away. I still could not entrust my soul to Christ. But I decided to become a catechumen in the Christian Church, in order to study its doctrines and so discover the truths they contained.

# THE PUZZLE OF GOD

*A*s I listened to Ambrose preach, I realised that many beliefs held by Christians, which I had found incredible and irrational, were in fact perversions of true Christian doctrine. In particular many Christians interpreted the verse 'God made men in his own image' as meaning that God had a bodily form. It was a joyful relief to find that for many years I had been barking, not against true Christian doctrine, but against a fiction. Yet I remained puzzled. If, as Ambrose said and the Scriptures taught, God is Spirit, and can in no way be confined to a human body, how can it be that man, who from head to foot is confined to a particular place, is 'made in his image'? At this time I could find no answer. My problem was that I could not firmly assent to anything unless I could prove it to be true. I wanted to be certain even of invisible things.

# ENCOUNTERING A BEGGAR

One day as I was walking along a street in Milan I saw a poor beggar. He was very merry and jovial, apparently under the influence of drink. It occurred to me that, whereas I in my desire for world renown, was anxious and miserable, the beggar without a care in the world was serenely happy. I shared the thought with my companions, observing that all our varied ambitions are really burdens on us: we strive to be happy and contented, but really the beggar, filled with cheap wine, enjoys greater happiness. They replied that the beggar's happiness was false, since it came from alcohol, whereas I desire true joy through achieving glory and renown. 'What glory?' I found myself asking. Joy based on worldly fame is as fake as the happiness of alcohol, and makes the head spin even faster. Worse still, the beggar can sleep off his drunkenness, while I carry my ambitions to bed, where they disturb my rest.

# SEXUAL CONFUSION

*I* had kept a mistress for several years. But gradually I felt that, as a sincere seeker after truth, I should marry. And so I decided to leave my mistress and find a wife of equal social status to my own. A friend Alipius urged me to reject marriage, saying that carnal pleasure, be it with a mistress or a wife, impedes the search for truth. I replied that many of the wisest men are married. Moreover there is great difference between the sexual pleasure he had experienced in furtive, snatched encounters and the joy of an honourable marriage. So with the help of my mother I began to search for a wife. Eventually a suitable young woman was found, but as she was two years short of the marriageable age, it was decided I should wait. I then explained my intentions to my mistress. She was heartbroken and angry, saying that I was treating her cruelly; and she returned to Africa, leaving our son with me in Milan. To my shame I now found myself unable to remain chaste, and took another lover.

# REFLECTIONS ON JESUS

*I* conceived of Jesus as a man of perfect wisdom, far above all other men. And his miraculous birth of a virgin showed how in him the spiritual had priority over the physical. But I could not yet understand the mystery which flowed from this, that in Jesus 'the word of God was made flesh'. All that I read in Scriptures – of his joys and sadnesses, of his miracles and sermons – showed him to be a perfect human. But I could not see how he was God in human flesh; rather I believed that he merely expressed the truth of God. Then one day, as I was reading Paul's Epistle to the Romans, a verse suddenly seemed to echo my despairing cries: 'My soul delights in the love of God, but I see another love at work in my body, which rejects God's love and makes me the slave of sin.' Then Paul asks 'Who shall deliver me from this body of death?' and replies 'Our Lord Jesus Christ!' At last I understood my predicament. Until then I had been puffed up with pride, insisting that I should understand truth before I believed it. Now I realised I must believe truth in order to understand it.

# BUT NOT YET

For so many years, since the age of nineteen, I had been searching for wisdom. Yet now I realised that through all this time I had in truth been holding back, unwilling to give up earthly pleasure. I had not been willing to put truth above all the pleasures and treasures of the world. And yet my entire adult life had been miserable, and even my youth was filled with anguish. I had been praying to God for moral purity, for chastity, but in my heart had been saying: 'Give me chastity, but not yet.' I was afraid that you would hear my prayers too soon, and deliver me instantly from my enslavement to lust. I wanted my desires to be glutted, not quenched.

# FINAL TURMOIL

*I*n my spiritual turmoil, I hurried out into the garden. I felt that I was going mad, that I was even dying. I was overwhelmed by misery. My whole soul was in a rage. I was gasping and groaning. I was desperately resisting the will of God, and yet all my bones cried out for him. I tore my hair. I struck my forehead. I clasped my knee, my body seized with anguish. I was still refusing to enter a true covenant with God, and yet I knew that soon I would be compelled to enter that covenant. I accused myself of my many sins, and I could feel the spiritual chains of those sins round my soul. God, in his severe mercy, was scourging me with fear and shame. I kept saying to myself, 'Let it happen now. Let it happen now'; and as I spoke I almost resolved to lay hold of God's grace and embrace it. But then I held back.

# THE VISION OF PURITY

*I* hung there, suspended between life and death. I was astonished at the power of my old evil habits, tugging at my soul. They whispered in my ear, 'If you take the step, you will never again experience the old pleasures. From this moment all our delights will be forbidden to you.' And, although I knew that, compared with eternal life, they were merely toys and vanities, their voices were still strong and seductive. But that strength was diverting. They no longer dared to speak to my face, but muttered behind my back. 'Do you ever think you can live without sinful joys?' the voice kept saying. Yet the sound grew fainter. I could see before me a new vision, of Purity herself. I trembled before her. She was beautiful, yet did not seek to entice me. She stretched out her hands, asking me to come forward. Around her were countless men and women, of all ages, who had already been received by her. She smiled, and said, 'Can you not do what all these have done? Cast yourself on God, and he will receive you and heal you.'

# THE MOMENT OF CONVERSION

*I* threw myself down under a fig tree, and tears flooded from my eyes like rivers. I cried out to God, 'How long, O God, how long? Will you be angry with me for ever? Do not remember my former sins.' Then I heard a voice, as if from a child, repeating in a sing-song manner, 'Take up and read, take up and read.' My bitter tears stopped. I was convinced the voice came from heaven, and was urging me to open the Bible and read the first verse I should find. So I walked over to a table where a Bible lay, and opened it. I saw the verse of the Epistle Paul: 'not in orgies and drunkenness, not in promiscuity and lust, not in anger and jealousy; but put on the Lord Jesus Christ, and make no provision for the flesh and its desires.' As soon as I read those words, a clear and constant light infused my soul, driving away the darkness of my former doubts. I knew I must turn from the old and put on the new. I went into the house and told my mother what had occurred. She was overjoyed, for her prayers for me were now answered.

# 2

## Doctrine

The teachings of Augustine, more than that of any other theologian, have defined orthodoxy, both among Catholics and among Protestants. Today many feel uneasy about his strict view of predestination and his uncompromising doctrine of original sin. But his theology is never arid or cold, but firmly rooted in his own spiritual experience. Thus even if one cannot wholly accept his conclusions, one can be moved by the insight that led him there.

# PRIMAL FREEDOM AND FINAL FREEDOM

*T*he first man had the ability not to sin, not to die, not to desert the good. This was the first freedom of the will, the ability not to sin. The final freedom will be a much greater freedom, the inability to sin. There was at first the power of perseverance, the ability not to desert the good. At the end there will be the joy of perseverance, the freedom to rejoice without inhibition.

from *Condemnation and Grace*

# THE STATE OF SIN

When there is sinful will in a man, then acts are done which would not be done if he did not so wish. These acts are voluntary, and thus the consequent punishment is just. Sin consists not in the actions themselves, but in the state of sin which motivates those actions. This is what is meant by saying that we are 'fallen': we are in a state of sin. For example, greed is not a fault belonging to money; it belongs to the man who through love of money abandons justice. Pride is not a fault belonging to the source of power, or even to power itself; it belongs to the soul which loves its own power, despising the claims of any higher power.

from *The City of God*

# ORIGINAL SIN

The source of sin is pride. Pride causes the soul to desert God to whom it should cling as the source of life, and causes the soul instead to imagine itself the source of its own life. Pride occurs when the soul loves itself too much, abandoning the unchanging goodness of God which it should love more than itself. Sin due to pride was voluntary, since if the will had remained steadfast in its love of the higher, unchanging good, which gives spiritual light and warmth, it would not have turned away to self-satisfaction, and so have been plunged into darkness and cold. Eve would not have believed the serpent nor Adam preferred his wife's wish to God's command. Yet man's pride did not result in his becoming utterly nothing. Rather it caused him to fall from that perfect state in which God had created him.

from *The City of God*

# FREEDOM AND GRACE

The first man did not have the grace to prevent him from willing evil. Rather he had the grace to enable him to be good, the grace without which he had not power to be good even with free will. Thus God's grace was always available to him, but receiving that grace depended on his free will. Free will is capable of evil, but incapable of good unless assisted by the all-powerful grace of God. Such was the first grace, given to the first Adam, and available to all men. The second grace that comes through the second Adam is far more powerful. This second grace ensures that man should will what is good, and love goodness so ardently that he may have victory over the will of the flesh. This second grace does not merely restore man's freedom to be good, but ensures that he is good. These two forms of grace must be distinguished. A man cannot live without food, but a supply of food does not ensure life if he wants to die. The first grace offers the probability of divine life: the second ensures that he receives it.

from *Condemnation and Grace*

# THE HUMANITY OF CHRIST

*T*he Son of God took on our human nature, and in it he endured all that belongs to the human condition. This is a remedy for mankind more powerful than we could imagine. Could any pride be cured, if the humility of God's Son does not cure it? Could any greed be cured, if the poverty of God's Son does not cure it? Or any anger, if the patience of God's Son does not cure it? Or any coldness, if the love of God's Son does not cure it? Or any fearfulness, if it is not cured by the resurrection of Christ? Let mankind raise its hopes, and recognise its own nature: let it observe how high a place it has in the works of God. Do not despise yourselves, you men: the Son of God answered mankind. Do not despise yourselves, you women: God's Son was born of a woman. Do not fear insults, pain or death: God's Son endured them to open for us the gate to eternal life.

from *Christian Struggle*

# CHOSEN FOR SALVATION

*T*hose who have not heard the gospel; those who after hearing it try to lead a better life but fall back; those who after hearing it refuse to come to Christ; those who could not hear the gospel because they died as infants – all these, in common with the whole human race, are condemned because of one man's sin. Yet men can be saved from the condemnation, not by their own merits, but through the grace of the Mediator – that is, they are justified freely by the blood of the second Adam. No one is set apart from this general condemnation, which results frcm the first Adam, unless he has been chosen to receive the grace of the Saviour. The chosen are chosen by grace, not because of their existing merits; for every merit is itself the result of grace.

from *Condemnation and Grace*

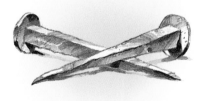

# TIME AND ETERNITY

*T*he Word of the Father, by whom all the cycles of time were made, entered time itself when he was made flesh in Bethlehem. With the Father the Word precedes all time, but by a human mother the Word chose a particular day to appear in time. The mother of men became man. The ruler of the stars was born beneath a star. The power that brings food from the earth sucked at the breast, and then ate bread. The one who is the Way to salvation walked along dusty roads. The eternal judge of all mankind was condemned by a mortal judge. The true vine wore a crown of thorns. The foundation of the earth itself was nailed to a tree. The source of all health was wounded in the side. The source of all joy suffered and died. He who was pure took upon himself the whole punishment of sin, that those who are saved, might go free. Through Christ time itself is made sacred, the stars, the plants, the trees and the earth made holy – and mankind is saved.

from *The Trinity*

# GOD OUR DEBTOR

*G*od is faithful. He made himself our debtor, not by accepting anything from us, but by promising us such great blessings. Even the promise was not enough. He chose to be bound by writing, through giving us the Scriptures; so when he began to fulfil his promises, we might follow in the Scriptures how he redeems his debts. He promised to men the divine nature; to morals, immortality; to sinners, justification; to castaways, a home of glory. He promised that men, created from dust, would become equal with the angels of God. And as a pledge of all these promises he gave his Son – a man who was divine, a mortal who was immortal, a man tempted by sin who remained sinless, a wanderer whose heart was always at home in heaven.

from *Discources on the Psalms*

# THE DEFORMITY OF CHRIST

*T*he deformity of Christ forms you. If he had not willed to be deformed, you would not have recovered the form which you had lost. Deformed he hung upon the cross. But his deformity is the source of our beauty. In this life let us hold fast to the deformity of Christ. Let us carry the sign of his deformity on our forehead. Let us not be ashamed of the deformity of Christ. Let us look with eyes of wonder at his deformity, for therein is the perfect justice of God.

from *Discourses on the Psalms*

# TRUE SACRIFICE

Every act which is aimed at uniting us to God is an act of sacrifice. An act of compassion may not be a true sacrifice if it is not done for the sake of God. It is the person not the act which constitutes the sacrifice. If a man has committed his life to God, then he himself becomes a sacrifice because he has laid himself on the altar of God. And every act which he performs, whether for his neighbour or for himself, is a true sacrifice. It follows from this that the Church itself is a universal sacrifice, offered to God through Christ who was both the highest priest and the first victim. From the universal sacrifice derives all individual acts of sacrifice.

from *The City of God*

## THE MEDICINE OF PRIDE

*L*et us always remember the humility whereby God was born of a woman and taken by mortal man to that most shameful death. If we hold that humility of God firmly in our hearts, it will be the supreme medicine for curing the cancer of our pride, and the sharpest knife to cut through the sin which binds us.

from *The Trinity*


## THE HOLY SPIRIT

*T*he Holy Spirit exists in unity and equality with the Father and the Son. Indeed he is that which unifies Father and Son because he is the bond of love between them. It is for this reason that there are three persons in God: the Father, the Son, and that which holds them together in perfect friendship. The Father loves the Son who is derived from him; the Son loves the Father from whom he is derived; and the Holy Spirit is their mutual love.

from *The Trinity*

## THE TRINITY IN MAN

When we speak of man as created in God's image, we see the Trinity reflected in human life. When I love something, there are three aspects to that love: there is my mind; there is the knowledge, within my mind of the object of love; and there is the love itself between my mind and the object. There is thus an image of the Trinity: mind, which is akin to the Father; knowledge which is the offspring of mind, and so is akin to the Son; and love which binds the mind with the knowledge it possesses. Just as the Son is not inferior to the Father, so knowledge is not inferior to its parents, mind, since they share the same essence. Equally, just as the Holy Spirit is equal to Father and Son, so love permeates both mind and knowledge, uniting itself with both.

from *The Trinity*

# SYMBOL AND SACRAMENT

We often say 'Easter coming', or 'it will be Passiontide in a few days', although it is long ago that the Lord suffered his passion, and that passion happened once for all. And on the Lord's day we say, 'Today Christ has risen', even though many years have passed since the resurrection. We are not, of course, lying when we make those statements, but rather we are saying that a particular day is similar to the day when those events took place, because it has the same position in the course of the year. In the same way, just as Christ was once sacrificed in his own person, so he is mystically sacrificed today throughout the year in the sacrament. The sacrament resembles that original event which it commemorates. And for this reason we give the sacrament the name of what it represents: we speak of the bread as Christ's body, and the wine as his blood.

from *Epistles*

# THE SACRAMENT OF NATURE

Ask the earth and the sea, ask the plains and the mountains, ask the sky and the clouds, ask the stars and the sun, ask the fish and the animals – and all will say, 'We are beautiful, because God has created us.' This beauty is their testimony to God. Ask too men and women, and they too know that their beauty came from God. Yet what is it that sees the beauty? What is it that can be enraptured by the loveliness of God's creation? It is the soul which discerns beauty. Indeed God fashioned men's souls so that they could discern the beauty of his handiwork. Yet the soul must not simply enjoy outward beauty, feasting its eyes on what God has made. For outward beauty fades and decays, it is constantly changing. The soul must understand all creation as a sacrament, an outward sign of the inward love of God. We must treat the natural world just as we treat the sacrament of bread and wine on God's altar: with respect and honour, with praise and adoration, but not as the first object of our love. The first object is not the creation but the Creator.

from *Sermons*

## THE USE OF SCRIPTURE

All scripture describes the coming of the Lord. The New Testament is hidden in the Old; the Old Testament is brought to light in the New. Those who are unspiritual have always failed to see this hidden meaning. Yet even before Christ those who were spiritual could find the Words of God hidden in the words of the prophets, and so through this understanding could be set free. In reading about Jesus Christ in the New Testament we should beware of forming in our mind a mental picture of him, because any picture of our own making will be far from the reality. In fact our picture will reflect our own limited understanding of perfect humanity. Instead our minds should be open, so the words of Jesus can speak directly to us. All that we read and know and believe about Christ is that he was the Word of God, born of a woman, and led to death to save us from our sin.

from *The Trinity*

# THE DEPTH OF SCRIPTURE

*T*here is such depth in the Christian Scriptures that, even if I studied them and nothing else from early boyhood to decrepit old age, with ample time and unflagging zeal, and with greater intellectual ability than I possess, I should still each day find something new within them. The basic truths necessary for salvation are easily found within the Scriptures. But even when one has accepted these truths, and is both pious and righteous in one's actions, there remain so many things which are under the great veil of mystery. Through reading the Scriptures, we are able to pierce this veil, and find in the Word, on the page, the deepest wisdom. The oldest, the ablest and the most eager student of Scripture will say at the end of each day: 'I have studied hard, but my studies are only just beginning.'

from *Epistle*

# THE PREACHER'S DILEMMA

*H*ave I spoken of God or sung his praises in any way worthy of his greatness? No, I have done nothing more than desire to speak; and, if I have said anything, it has fallen far short of what I wanted to say. God is beyond words. Indeed, one should not even say that he is beyond words, because that itself is an attempt to describe him. So those who are called to preach and write about God are caught in a curious conflict about words. If God cannot be spoken of or praised in words, then our sermons and our books are mere dust; only silence can be worthy of him. And yet if we say nothing we cannot convey to others the faith which God has granted us. The answer is that, although nothing worthy of God can be spoken, God has allowed us to express our faith and rejoice and sing in the medium of words. Yet we must always remember that the word 'God' is merely a sound, conveying nothing of his nature.

from *Treatise on St. John's Gospel*

# CLASSES OF TRUTH

*T*here are three classes of truth. Firstly, there are the facts of history, describing the temporal activities of mankind. These are understood with the heart, through identifying one's own feelings with those of others, since the motives of all people are in essence the same. Secondly there are the facts of science, describing the workings of nature. These we understand with the intellect, since the laws of Nature are logical. Thirdly there are the truths of God, describing both God in Himself, and God in His relationship with that which He has created. These can only be understood by the soul; as for the soul to understand God it must be pure. The first two classes of truth make no moral demands on mankind. The third class of truth can only be grasped by those who first keep God's commandments.

from *Diverse Questions*

## FAITH AND UNDERSTANDING

*I*f we are to understand the mysteries and secrets of the Kingdom of God, we must have faith in God. Some people, who call themselves rational, say that they cannot believe anything before they understand it. Those people shall attain neither faith nor understanding. Faith is the first step towards understanding; and understanding is the reward of faith. Certainly faith arises in part from what we see: the first disciples saw Christ and had faith, just as our faith arises from meeting Christ in Scripture. But seeing is not understanding. We shall only understand Christ if we follow him with all our heart. Our outward eyes, which are windows on the world, see the figure of Christ; but it is our inward eyes, the windows on truth, which understand him.

from *Sermons*

# 3

# Spirituality

Augustine's knowledge of the Scriptures was profound, and he regarded his spiritual teaching as an exposition of the spirituality of the Bible. Hence his greatest devotional works were commentaries and also sermons based on a scriptural text. He regarded the books of the Bible not as neat packages of truth, but as vivid accounts of men's relationship with God, in which anguish and doubt are as important as joy and faith.

## THE SUPREME GOOD

To seek the supreme good a man must act with justice and charity. To act justly a man must love God with all his heart, his mind and his soul. To love God totally the soul must be pure and strong, remaining faithful to God in times of trouble, watchful against all dishonesty and fraud. In this way man will not merely find the supreme good, he will himself become like the supreme good – because he will be transfigured in the image of God.

*from Catholic Church*


## DESCENDING INTO SELF

Descend into yourself. Go beneath your clothing, beneath your flesh. Go right into the secret chamber of your soul. If you cannot come close to your own soul, you can never come close to God. It is not your body, but your soul which has been created in the image of God. Seek God within your soul, for in understanding your own soul you shall recognise its Creator.

*from Treatise on St. John's Gospel*

# DESIRE FOR GOD

*I*f you are to come to God it is not sufficient to be drawn to him by your own free will; you must be drawn by delight as well. What does this mean, to be drawn by delight? There is in every heart a desire for the bread of heaven. This desire delights in the truth, in holiness, in eternal life – in all things belonging to Christ. There is no necessity, no compulsion to seek God; you will only seek him if you are prompted by this desire, and so are drawn towards God by sheer pleasure. Show me a lover, and he will understand what I mean. Show me someone who is hungry, or who is travelling abroad and longs to be back home; they will know what I mean. But show me a man without feeling, and he will not know what I am talking about. If the delights of love can draw a man to a woman, if hunger and loneliness can impel a man to travel miles in search of food and shelter, how much more will desire for truth and holiness impel a man to seek God.

from *Treatise on St. John's Gospel*

## PRAYING WITHOUT CEASING

*I*t is your heart's desire which is your prayer; and if your desire continues uninterrupted, so too does your prayer continue. This is what is meant by 'praying without ceasing': it is the uninterrupted prayer of the heart. Whatever else you are doing, so long as your heart desires God, then you never cease to pray. So if you want to pray without ceasing, you must always desire God. The continuance of that desire is the continuance of prayer.

from *Discourses on the Psalms*

## MAN'S CHIEF WORK

*M*an's chief work is to praise God. And he in turn will satisfy your deepest desires by his beauty, inspiring you to praise him with ever greater devotion. If you dislike praising God, and find excuses for avoiding it, it is because you love yourself too much. Be dissatisfied with yourself. See your satisfaction in him who made you, and only then find satisfaction in yourself as part of his creation.

from *Discourses on the Psalms*

# IMAGE OF GOD

*D*elight in God as he is, not as you would wish him to be. In our perversity we try to make God like ourselves, rather than know him as he is. Instead we should try to make ourselves like God, living in perfect harmony with him. We must like ourselves as we are, in order to be loved and transformed by God.

from *Sermons*

# GOD EVERYWHERE

*D*o not think of God in particular places. Wherever you go, he is present. If you are good in your actions, you will be pleased at his presence; but if you are evil, then you will be fearful, and pretend he is not there. God resides in your heart and your conscience, encouraging you to do good, and upsetting your inward peace when you do evil. Wishing to do evil you may lock yourself in your house, hoping that no one will see you. And you may still be so frightened of detection, that you lock yourself in your heart, and imagine the evil. But God is in your house and in your heart. You cannot escape from yourself, so you cannot escape from God. So do not try to flee from God. Flee to him.

from *Discourses on the Psalms*

## THE PUZZLE OF PRAYER

**W**hy does the Lord urge us to pray, when he knows what we need before we ask him? This can seem puzzling, and can make prayer seem like wasted effort. But prayer is not merely expressing our present desires. Its purpose is to exercise and train our desires, so that we want what he is preparing to give. His gift is very great, and we are small vessels for receiving it. So prayer involves widening our hearts to God. We pray to God at fixed times of the day in order to remember our desire for God. And we pray in words, which in themselves are mere symbols, in order to focus our hearts on the inner truths behind the words.

from *Letter to Proba*

# THE RIVER OF TIME

We can love the world, or love God. If we love the world, there is no room in our heart for the love of God. We cannot both love God, who is eternal, and love the world, which passes away. You ask, 'Why should I not love the world, since God made it?' Brethren, if your love is directed towards the world, you will love the world for its own sake, not for the sake of its Creator. There is nothing wrong with loving created things, unless they are loved for themselves. You must choose: either love the things of time, and pass away with them; or love God, and live forever with him. Time is like a river sweeping onwards. But, like a tree planted in the water, there is Jesus Christ. When you feel yourself drifting towards the rapids, reach out for the tree; when you feel tempted by the world, hold fast to Christ. For our sake he entered time, but he did not cease to be eternal.

from *Treatise on the First Epistle of St. John*

# THE PRICE OF LOVE

*T*he price of wheat is copper coins. The price of land is silver coins. The price of jewels is gold coins. The price of love is yourself. You may struggle and save to purchase a farm, to buy a beast of burden to pull the plough; and when you own your farm, you work hard to build a fine house. But if you want love, you must struggle within your soul, and you must work hard to build generosity within your heart. Just as you spend all your money buying a farm, so you spend your whole self to find God. Are you frightened of such a high price? Are you anxious about the hardship you must endure to afford the price of love? Remember to live without love is ultimately far worse, for it leads to utter misery. And remember the One who demands that you give yourself is the One who made you. God does not demand this price for his own profit, because nothing can be added to God. He demands that you give to him all that you are and all that you possess, in order that he may give to you something more precious than the finest jewel – eternal life.

from *Sermons*

## FEAR AND LOVE

*W*hen a person becomes a Christian his heart is enlarged, because he takes delight in justice. This delight is a gift from God. God does not make our hearts shrink with fear of punishment, but enlarges our heart with the knowledge of his love. Hence we take pleasure in being generous to others, we enjoy seeing the hungry fed and the thirsty given drink. For we know that God has given his Son to take the punishment we deserve, and hence cast out all fear in those who put their faith in Christ.

from *Sermons*


## LOVE OF GOD AND NEIGHBOUR

*T*he love of God is the first and greatest commandment. But love of our neighbour is the means by which we obey it. Since we cannot see God directly, God allows us to glimpse him in our neighbour. By loving our neighbours we purge our eyes for seeing God. Love, therefore, your neighbour; and you shall discover that in loving your neighbour you come to know God.

from *Treatise on St. John's Gospel*

# FAILURE AND HOPE

We try to keep vigil, and yet we fall asleep. We try to fast, and yet our minds remain remain obsessed with food and drink. We try to remain standing during worship, but we get exhausted and sit down. Whatever we do to make ourselves better, we seem to fail. How then can we here on earth find peace amidst so many troubles, desires, wants, failures? Is there perfect peace? Where there is mortality, can there be peace? Is it only in death that we may find peace? In death we shall enjoy pure peace as sons of God, loving one another, seeing one another filled with the divine spirit, united in God's love. God shall be our common object of vision, our common possession, our common peace. Yet this future hope can to some degree be our present joy. The things which God shall bestow upon us in heaven are in part offered to us now. He is our peace now because in heaven he will be our full and perfect peace. Our job, our peace, our rest, the end of all our troubles is none but God.

from *Discourses on the Psalms*

# TROUBLES ON EARTH

*I*f prison is the cause of your trouble, you try to get out of prison. If fever is the cause of your trouble, you try to get well. If hunger is the cause of your trouble, you seek food. If poverty is the cause of your trouble, you seek wealth. If staying away is the cause of your trouble, you travel home. Yet in all these troubles you should seek God. You should not put him away from your troubles, but within them. God can only relieve your troubles if you in your anxiety cling to him. In truth trouble should not be thought of as this thing or that thing in particular, for this whole life on earth involves trouble. And it is through the troubles of this earthly pilgrimage that we find God.

from *Discourses on the Psalms*

# HOPE IN GOD

*L*et the Lord your God be your hope. Hope for nothing else from the Lord your God, but let the Lord your God himself be your hope. Many people hope to gain riches from God, others hope for worldly honour; in other words their hope is in what God may give, not in God himself. But you should forget all the gifts that God may bestow, and seek only God himself. Leave other things behind and stretch your hands to him. It is he who brings you back on the right path when you stray. It is he who is leading you to your goal. Where in the end do worldly desires lead you? For example a man might desire a farm, a large estate; and then when he has obtained it, he would shut out his neighbours. Soon he would begin to desire his neighbours' estates; and when he had obtained them, he would want to possess the whole land, and then the world itself – and finally even want to possess heaven itself. Such desires can never be satisfied. So desire only God, and your heart will be fulfilled.

from *Discourses on the Psalms*

## SELF-GIVING LOVE

When by God's gift we live by the true faith, God himself is present, to enlighten our minds, to overcome our lusts, and to bear our afflictions. This happens when we love him for his own sake, with no thought of reward. But such self-giving love cannot be achieved by our own efforts; it is a miracle from God. When, however, a man is pleased with himself, when he surrenders to the desires of his pride, then his love for God will be tainted with desire for reward. And the mind remains dull, lusts remain rampant, and afflictions intolerable.

from *Against Julian*

## CHRIST BEFORE US

When we work in a spirit of love, we are never working alone. Rather we are co-working with God who gives us strength, and whose love gives us courage. When we are sick, we need never be alone in our misery. His hand is upon our fevered brow, as his healing grace is restoring our vigour. Wherever we go, whatever we do, he goes ahead of us, beckoning us onwards, and showing us the way of righteousness.

from *Nature and Grace*

## EYE OF FAITH

*H*usband and wife love what they can see in each other; but if in every respect they hide themselves from each other, then there will be fear and suspicion. God is invisible to us, and yet we are called to love and trust him, not fear and suspect him. That is why we depend on the gift of faith. It is through the eyes of faith that we see God, and so trust him. And the eye of faith sees God far more clearly than the natural eyes of husband and wife can see one another. That is why we can love God with greater passion than we can love a spouse.

from *Holy Virginity*


## TESTING OF FAITH

*W*hen we live in Christ we are tested. Just as he died on the cross, we must die to pride. Just as he was mocked, we must be insulted for our faith. Just as he was abandoned by his friends, so we shall feel lonely in our loyalty to him. In that loneliness we shall find eternal love. In that mockery we shall find eternal honour. In that death, we shall find eternal life.

from *Discourses on the Psalms*

# PEACE

Peace shall be your gold. Peace shall be your silver. Peace shall be your God. Peace shall be to you whatever you most desire. On the earth gold cannot be silver, wine cannot be bread, and the rage of the sun cannot quench thirst. But the peace of God can be all things to you. He is the eternal bread that satisfies your hunger for ever. He is the eternal wine that quenches your thirst for ever. He is your light, so you shall never be plunged in darkness. He shall hold you up, so you shall never fall. He shall possess you whole and entire. And in him everything in heaven and on earth belongs to you. In him there is fullness of life.

from *Discourses on the Psalms*

# 4

# *Prayers*

In every collection of prayers those of Augustine loom large. And his phrases are echoed in numerous prayers, composed by others. Augustine rarely wrote a prayer for public, or even private use. Rather, his spiritual and theological writings are peppered with paragraphs addressed directly to God; and it is these which have been extracted and included in prayer books ever since.

## WHO, O LORD?

*W*ho, O Lord, will allow me to rest in you?
Who will allow you to enter my heart and
make me drunk with love for you? Who will
make me forget my wicked ways, and embrace you,
the only source of goodness? Have mercy on me, that
I may speak to you. What am I to you, that you should
command me to love you? Say to my soul, 'I am your
salvation.' Open my ears to your voice, open my eyes
to your face, open my heart to receive your grace.


## O GOD, WHO KNOWS OUR NECESSITIES

*O* God, you know our necessities before we ask,
and our ignorance in asking. Let us be free from
all anxious thoughts for the morrow; make us
content with your good gifts; and confirm our faith
that, as we seek your kingdom, you will not deny us
any good thing.

## O GOD, YOU ARE CLOSE

*O* God, you are close to all those who call upon you in truth. You are truth itself, the source of eternal life. Instruct us with your widsom and teach us your love, that we may know the truth at work in it. We ask this in the name of Jesus, in whom truth was made manifest.

## BLESSED ARE YOUR SAINTS

*B*lessed are your saints, O Lord, who have travelled over the rough sea of this life, and have reached the harbour of eternal peace and joy. Watch over us who are still on the dangerous voyage. Our ship is frail, and the ocean is wide. But in your mercy you have set us on our course with your Son as our pilot, guiding us towards the everlasting shore of peace, the quiet haven of our hectic desire.

## O LORD, YOU WERE RICH

*O* Lord, you were rich, yet for our sakes you became poor; and you have promised that whatever we do for the least of your brethren is done for you. Give us grace to be always willing to serve the needs of others, and so extend the blessings of your kingdom throughout the world.


## ALL THINGS LIVE IN YOU

*A*ll things live in you, O God. You command us to seek you, and you are always ready to be found. To know you is life, to serve you is freedom, to praise you is joy. We bless and adore you, worship and magnify you, thank and love you.

## OUR HEARTS ARE COLD

*O*ur hearts are cold, warm them with your selfless love. Our hearts are sinful; cleanse them with your precious blood. Our hearts are weak; strengthen them with your joyous Spirit. Our hearts are empty; fill them with your holy presence. Our hearts belong to you, Lord Jesus; possess them always and only for yourself.

## IN YOU WE LIVE

*I*n you we live and move and have our being. You have made us for yourself, so our souls are restless until they rest in you. Grant us purity of heart and strength of purpose, that no selfish passion may hinder us from knowing your will, and no weakness from doing it.

## LET MY SOUL PRAISE YOU

*L*et my soul praise you that it may love you. Your whole creation sings your praise. Man sings your praise with hymns and psalms. Animals and plants praise you with their beauty. Your whole creation lifts up our hearts, that we may glimpse the glory of heaven.

## DESCEND INTO MY HEART

*D*escend into my heart, O Holy Spirit, and lighten the dark corners of this wretched dwelling. Pierce the gloom, with your joyful beams, dwell in that soul that longs to be your temple; water the barren soil, overrun with weeds and thistles, making it fruitful with dew from heaven. O come, refresh my faint and languid spirit. O come, guide this lost soul tossed about on the stormy seas of this world, and bring me safely to the haven of your love.

## YOU, LORD, ARE THE LIGHT

*Y*ou, Lord, are the light of minds that know you, the joy of hearts that love you, and the strength of wills that serve you. Grant us so to know you that we may truly love you, and so to love you that we may fully serve you, for to serve you is perfect freedom.

## WATCH THIS NIGHT

*W*atch this night, O Lord, over those who are awake, and watch over those who sleep. Watch over those who weep. Tend those who are sick. Give rest to those who are weary. Bless those who are dying. Soothe those who are in pain. Have mercy on all who are in any way distressed.

## COME LORD, SET US ON FIRE

Come, Lord, set us on fire. Clasp us close to your bosom. Seduce us with your beauty. Enchant us with your fragrance. Let us love you.